There are far too many of us who are going through life afraid, sad, depressed, worried or feeling guilty about something we've said or done. There are too many of us who are dealing with daily conflicts or living in uncomfortable situations – both physically and emotionally. There are too many of us who are simply putting up with the ordeals of every-day life and are maybe wondering if things will ever change – if this is really "as good as it gets".

We are 100 percent convinced that with very few exceptions, every one of our lives CAN BE BETTER! We believe that it's possible for every one of us to do better – to be happier, feel less stress, have fewer hassles, have more fun and overall, ENJOY LIFE MORE.

And no, we are not saying that we can all become millionaires or that we can all have the "fantasy" life we've been drooling over. Life's just not like that for most of us. What we are saying though is that no matter who you are, what you do, or what your life has been like up to now, it CAN BE BETTER!

If your life is giving you something less than you'd like, if you're ready to make a few changes and improvements here and there, "Just Go For It!" can be one more step toward a truly enjoyable life – and will offer at least a few smiles along the way.

I wish you an absolutely terrific life!

Gene

Dedicated to all of my "teachers" who have brought me to this point in my life and to all of those who share their love so freely with me

JUST
GO
FOR
IT!

First Edition Copyright 2004, Second Edition Revised Copyright 2005 by Gene Simmons

NuPathz

http://www.nupathz.com/

Bringing You a New Perspective on Life!

Contents

DON'T QUIT

When things go wrong,
  as they sometimes will,
When the road you're trudging
  seems all up hill,
When the funds are low,
  and the debts are high,
And you want to smile,
  but you have to sigh,
When care is pressing
  you down a bit,
Rest if you must
  but don't you quit...
Success is failure
  turned inside out.
The silver tint
  of the clouds of doubt.
And you never can tell
  how close you are,
It may be near
  when it seems so far
So stick to the fight
  when you're hardest hit,
It's when things seem worst,
  *that **you must not quit.***

  Unknown

In the Beginning

For every journey, there's a starting point – and this looks like as good of a place as any to begin. To get us going, here are four "Truths" that I believe can help transport any of us from where we are today to a more productive, enjoyable lifestyle.

1. The stuff we've learned so far in our little lives has led us right to where we are today – as good, bad or indifferent as it may be.
2. The more we know about why we are the way we are, the better our chances for making some super improvements in our lives.
3. The more we can back off from our day-to-day survival mode of living to see if we can at least catch a glimpse of the "big picture", the better our chances are of understanding ourselves, of appreciating this great creation we're a part of – and of really beginning to enjoy life.
4. The more we can open our mind to the infinite possibilities life has to offer, the better our chances are of…well, see previous #3.

OK, enough of the numbering/list silliness. I'm sure you have the idea. Let me make one major point before we go any further. The intent of this material is not to persuade anyone to do anything differently than they have been doing all along. Really! (Trust me..?) The whole purpose for doing this is to encourage folks to just take the time to THINK – about stuff they don't normally think about – and in the process maybe LEARN some really cool stuff that actually can make their lives easier and more fun. I know that what I'm writing has – and is – working for me. Will it work for you too? Probably, but who knows…

Yeah, I know. This is a really sucky motivational technique, but frankly, I'd rather be up front (honest) than try to blow smoke up your collective rears and attempt to convince you that this is the greatest concept since sex. I think you're probably all too smart for that (OK, with maybe a few exceptions, but I'd still rather be honest).

I've been reading, studying and thinking about the "Truths" listed above for a long time. Here's the way it worked out. About 20 years ago (after diligent study), I started to feel that I had a pretty good handle on why I was the way I was – and what life was all about. Around 15 years ago, I knew I was getting pretty darned smart. Ten years ago, I was sure I was an expert. Five years ago, I knew it all and was ready to take my esteemed knowledge to the world (for a nominal fee, of course). Now…right now…I am thoroughly convinced that I don't know Diddley Squat. (There's that sucky motivational technique again. Dang…)

That also just happens to be one of life's premier lessons. As we mature and learn, we realize that all of the "facts" of life that we have stored in our little brain are frequently not so much facts as just possibilities. And thankfully, learning that then enables us to open our minds to a wonderful, fascinating world filled with other possibilities that we had never before considered. As a result, I'm passing along some of these "possibilities' in the off chance that it might help someone out and maybe help make his/her life a little more enjoyable.

Hopefully as we go down the road, you'll find a few things that can help you do whatever you want to do. Oh yeah, one more thing. Don't take yourself and any of this stuff too seriously. Life's too short for that. And besides, too much thinkin' can turn your brain to mush – and none of us have all that much extra gray matter that we can afford to squander it away…

To get us started, here's a quick review (or maybe for some of you, some brand new info/concepts) of just why the heck we are the way we are. Why we think and act the way we do. Why is this important? Because if we don't know how we got to be the way we are, there ain't any way in hell we're going to be able to open up our pea brains to get the information we could use to help make any changes in the way we do things so our lives will be better and maybe a little more enjoyable.

First of all, we all know that it is our parents/caregivers "fault" that we are the way we are. I know of folks who have become really good at carrying this concept to the extreme. They have managed to slog their way through life in a victim mode (the old "woe-is-me" syndrome) without taking a lick of responsibility for any of their thoughts or actions. Too bad, 'cause things aren't apt to get any better for them unless they do some quick learnin'.

Not that these good people are 100% wrong. Our genetic composition that has been so carefully constructed (or not) complements of our egg supplier and sperm donor in hopefully a heat of semi-frenzied passion (how's that for a new picture of Mom & Dad?) has provided the foundation for our physical and physiological characteristics including our brain assembly and functioning. Their actions and words toward (or just around) us provided the initial programming for our thought patterns and the resulting responses/reactions to the subsequent events in our lives.

The rest of our mental programming is mostly the result of environmental influences (everything that we've seen, heard, touched, smelled or tasted) from that time on. We've managed to use most of this input to reinforce the concepts and thinking patterns that were established in our younger years. I've heard that our values, etc., are pretty well set before we hit the teenage years. Good chance that for most of us this is about right.

Does this mean that all the information we've received has been complete, accurate, unbiased or even useful? Heck no! Some of it has even been downright detrimental and self-limiting. And that applies to just about every single one of us no matter how great our childhood and formative years appear to have been.

The end result of our genetics, experiences and life-long programming (or establishment of mental filters if that thought is more comfortable to you) is that we all are the proud possessors of our own personal values, beliefs, thought patterns and techniques for dealing with the events in our lives. Some of this stuff works fine and as a result our lives are pretty cool and in general, quite enjoyable. Some of it doesn't work as well and our lives are generally pretty sucky. Cool or sucky, one thing that you can about put money on is the rigidity of our programming. It's one of those "By dang, I am the way I am and I'm darned well gonna stay that way!"

The only way for us to get out of our rut so that we can move on toward the life we'd really like to enjoy is to change our thinking habits. It's time to step away, even for just a few minutes, from the pressures of our daily lives to think about what we're doing, why we're doing it – and to think about if this is the way we really want the remainder our lives to be. Worth doing, don'tcha think?

Conscious, Subconscious or Just Unconscious?

For those of you who are just now gingerly stepping into the self improvement arena and aren't too sure about whether or not this mental programming concept is a possibility, here are a couple of examples that might help.

Just for the heck of it, let's say our brains function on at least two different levels. Apart from automatically controlling respiration, digestion and all of the other functions necessary for us to keep living, let's imagine that we have one section that we consciously use to analyze stuff and make reasonably logical observations and decisions. We'll call this the "conscious" section. The other section, which we'll refer to as the "subconscious", acts like a dumb old computer and blindly processes and stores the "facts" that we feed into it. It then automatically refers to these "facts" as we cruise through life and uses them to influence (control?) the rest of our thoughts, opinions or actions. Information that does not mesh easily with (or is not consistent with) the "facts" that are already stored are quickly, automatically rejected as false. Information that blends with that which is in storage is readily accepted and used to reinforce the previous programming.

A simple example. When we were born, we had no idea what the word "no" meant. After repeated reprimands and hearing the word "no" coupled with slaps on the hand or swats on the butt, we learned that "no" meant pain and that our caregivers didn't want us to continue to pull the kitty's tail or eat out of the dog's dish. This important information was dutifully stored in our subconscious. We no longer had to think about what "no" meant. We just knew. Whether we then consciously forced ourselves past this knowledge to do those things we weren't supposed to do was up to us. A separate decision. But we still automatically knew what "no" meant. We still do.

One more example. Think about your signature. When you first attempted to make those lines that represented your name, it was really an effort. You had to consciously think about what you were doing and actually drew the lines that formed the letters. Now whaddaya do? Zip – blap – you're done! It's all automatic. The programming (yeah, this is like a habit thing) is doing the job for you. Just as a sidelight here, watch an elderly person write their signature. It's sliding back to the drawing mode again, isn't it? And what happens if you try to write your signature with your other hand? With very few exceptions, we have to work really hard to get past our programming to draw something that resembles the scrawl of a five year old.

The bottom line? It appears to me (yeah, this is my pro-gramming – or maybe even reprogramming – talking) that our subconscious has stored and reinforced all kinds of "facts" that heavily influence our perceptions of life, our values, our prejudices, our beliefs and how we respond (or automatically react) to the multitude of events that occur daily. And – just as it is difficult for us to switch hands when writing our signature, it is not at all easy to switch our perceptions and modify our pro-gramming so that we are receptive to suggestions and alternate ways of thinking. It is not easy to see that with perhaps only a few small changes in our thought patterns, our lives could be so much better and so much more enjoyable than they are now. It just ain't easy!

But it is possible! Maybe we oughtta think about it…

Bad Words...

For today class, to reinforce the concept of mental programming, I thought we would turn our attention to the bad words of the world. As an introductory quiz, please take a clean sheet of paper and in the next 30 seconds write down every bad word or short phrase you can think of. Abbreviations are permissible. I'll wait...

Finished? OK, lemme check... Whoa! Some of you did really good! You have listed some words that I hadn't even thought of. On the other hand, there are a few of you who have apparently been leading excessively sheltered lives. You really should get out more.

Did you enjoy that little exercise? Sort of like a mental laxative, huh? OK, for those of you who thought it was completely stupid, I agree with you totally. In fact, my clean sheet of paper is still...yep, completely clean. (For those of you who are leaping ahead and already see the full logic in this, you're just going to have to chill out for a couple of minutes while I bring everyone else up to speed.)

For the rest of you, my paper is completely clean because...are you ready for this..? There is no such a thing as a "bad" word! THINK about it! Words are just combinations of letters or sounds that we humans use to represent a concept. They're just squiggly little lines on a piece of paper or computer screen. They're just varying little sound waves that wiggle the tiny hairs in our middle ear. We see the squiggles and hear the sounds – and translate them into something semi-meaningful. We produce the squiggles and sounds to communicate with other humans. With a little luck, we will have already generally agreed on the meanings of these symbols and communications will occur.

Words carry only the meaning or connotation that we have assigned to them. We consider them to be "good" or "bad" because our parents, teachers, society, etc., have told us – sometimes through painful reinforcement – that they <u>are</u> good or bad. We individually learn and are essentially programmed to intuitively "know" which words are bad. Our subconscious is programmed to apply strong negative connotations to some of these "bad" words. And yes, to be fair here, we are also pro-grammed to apply strong positive connotations to many of the "good" words.

We set limits on who can say many of these words and where these words can be used. Think about it. When was the last time you heard a minister say "shit" in front of the congregation? And yet, this is one of most expressive words in the language and is commonly used effectively to express a wide range of emotions. The language in the locker room is considerably dif-ferent than that used in the board room. The language used in the bedroom is usually different than that used at the dining room table – or in front of our kids. We normally use language that is acceptable within our immediate environment and acceptable to us personally.

Personal acceptance and any resulting connotation <u>is</u> ultimately an individual thing. No, I'm not advocating that we all fill our daily conversations with those words that are not acceptable in our immediate situation/environment. What I am saying is that the personal – and sometimes emotional – impact that words have on us is the result of our life-long programming and that in reality, the power of words – all words – is limited to that which we personally bestow upon them. Maybe some of us should consider reducing that power level a couple of notches. Just a thought.

Our Life – Our Choice…

OK, maybe that's a bit of an over-generalization but it applies most of the time. Basically, what I am saying is that we are what we are because that's what we've decided to be. We live where we live, do what we do and think what we think because that's we've decided to do. Yes, I understand that there are some illnesses and other stuff that happens that tends to force us into a particular mode of operation. But by the same token, how we function within our situation and how we deal with the things we need to deal with is always our decision.

This takes us right back to one of my foundation principles - we believe what we believe because of our personal programming. Our present perception (whatever it is) of what is written in the preceding paragraph is absolutely correct based on our life experiences, input – and programming. Does that mean that there are no incorrect opinions and this is one of those "I'm OK, you're OK so let's hold hands and sing something" things? Oh, heck no! This just means that we all have our personal reasons for doing what we do and thinking what we think.

Unfortunately, none of us – repeat, none of us has been fortunate enough to get one hundred percent accurate and un-biased information and input into our little pea brains as we've trudged through life. As a result, we're all playing our life game with a few cards missing from our deck. It's almost a sure bet that we'll never find all of 'em, but I think the sporty thing to do is to do our best to search out at least a couple more cards before we revert back to our basic earth elements. And yeah, we'll count the Jokers as worth keeping. (Maybe they're really the ones we oughtta look for first! Just a thought.) Note: For those of you who are presently holding a partial deck that is only giving you a Jack high poker hand, heck that's good enough to open. Hang in there and keep playing!

Now that we've come out of the closet and admitted that we're all screwed up to some extent, let's get back to the initial subject. Our life – and nearly all of its components – is the result of our decisions that have been heavily influenced (or even controlled) by our programming. And yeah, we may have also been heavily influenced by other factors – namely people – but unless someone is holding a gun to our heads to "force" us to do what we're doing, the reason we're here at this point in our lives is because of the decisions we've made. Even with a gun aimed at our noggins, we still have a couple of options to choose from, don't we?

For those of us who are completely satisfied with the way our lives are going in every little detail – we should take a lot of satisfaction in knowing that we have been extremely fortunate to have been able to make some very beneficial decisions. Back up a second here. The biggie word in the last sentence was "satisfied". I didn't say "happy". We can be generally happy with the way things are going in our lives – and still not be satisfied. The way I look at it, if we have just one small thing we'd like to do differently or better, then we're not completely satisfied. Cool! That keeps us from joining the walking dead and trudging down our rut to the slime pit.

For those of us who are not completely satisfied with every little detail in our lives (that'd be me), we really should seriously consider doing something about it! And that brings me to the main point of this little discussion. To be able to do something about our lives, to make the changes and improvements that we feel we would like to make, we need to first say the following words:

"I (insert your name here) hereby take full responsibility for all aspects of my life. I am personally fully accountable for who I am, what I believe and what I have accomplished - and will accomplish in my life."

Of course, you can expand that if you want, to include never blaming anyone else for your situation, to understand and respect the rights of others to have any opinion they want because now you know why they think and believe the way they do, to not take stuff so seriously because everyone is doing whatever they think is the best thing to do at the time, that we're all a little goofy and that helps make this world a really interesting place to live and that you're going to do your best to take some time for yourself every day to think about cool stuff and just relax and that you're going to chill out and have some fun and enjoy life more. (Whew, I need to take a deep breath!)

Once we can accept full responsibility for our lives and what we are, only then are we capable of moving on toward our goals and a truly enjoyable lifestyle. Well worth doing, I'd say.

If a Dog was the Teacher

If a dog was the teacher, you would learn stuff like.....

When loved ones come home, always run to greet them.
Never pass up the opportunity to go for a joyride.
Allow the experience of fresh air and the wind in your face to be
    pure ecstasy.
When it's in your best interest, practice obedience.
Let others know when they've invaded your territory.
Take naps. Stretch before rising.
Run, romp, and play daily.
Thrive on attention and let people touch you.
Avoid biting when a simple growl will do.
On warm days, stop to lie on your back on the grass.
On hot days, drink lots of water and lie under a shady tree.
When you're happy, dance around and wag your entire body.
No matter how often you're scolded, don't buy into the guilt
    thing and pout... run right back and make friends.
Delight in the simple joy of a long walk.
Eat with gusto and enthusiasm. Stop when you have had enough.
Be loyal.
Never pretend to be something you're not.
If what you want lies buried, dig until you find it.
When someone is having a bad day, be silent, sit close by and
    nuzzle them gently.

And finally, never trust anyone until you sniff their butt.

Scary Stuff

Life can be downright scary - sometimes more than others. Probably all of us are wandering through life afraid of something – maybe a situation, an event or other people. Because we're individuals with differing backgrounds and experiences, our fears vary from person to person. Some people have no problem parachuting from an airplane while others of us think that's a really dumb idea and our insides get all stirred up even thinking about it. Some of us rather enjoy standing in front of a group of people teaching or just BS'ing while others of us toss our cookies immediately at the idea.

So how did we learn to be skeer'd of all this different stuff? Even though there are likely some foundation survival, self-preservation instincts in all of us, most of the rest of our fears come from our life learning experiences – our programming. If your mother dove under the bed every time there was an electrical storm, there is an excellent chance that you'll be tempted to do exactly the same thing. If your older sibling was deathly afraid of the monsters in the closet or under the bed, there's a good chance that you will have absorbed this apprehension. We've learned what we've learned and dutifully filed it away in our subconscious. Then, unless we've been really aware of what has happened to start up these fears in the first place, we've probably put out a bunch of effort to make sure they've been solidly reinforced.

It's not uncommon for us to get things twisted up, however. Here's a quick example. Regress to childhood for a minute (for those of you who make a habit of living there, this should be a snap). Since as early as you can remember, Uncle Harold has always showed up at your house at least once a week. Uncle Harold looks funny – he's short, fat, balding and smokes super stinky cigars. Uncle Harold is a real pain in the rear. Every time he gets close to you, he either pinches you really hard – or gives you a painful swat. Uncle Harold is an obnoxious, aggravating butthead. You do everything you can to keep your distance from

Uncle Harold, but he always finds you. Your life is miserable when he's around.

So did our stupid subconscious simply file away the information that Uncle Harold is a bad person and that we hate to be around him? No way. In time, our wonderful, well-meaning memory bank extrapolated this basic concept to **"Short, fat, balding men are dangerous! Keep away! Keep away! Do not trust them! And watch out for cigar smokers, too! Danger! Danger!"** It would take more than a few positive interactions with a super nice, short, fat, bald guy before we decided it was OK to do some reprogramming.

Is it any wonder we're screwed up? Think of all the misinformation we've been subjected to over the years – and how easily we have been able to reinforce this BS. Some of our programming has led us now to firmly believe (and by doggies we can prove all this with examples) that Hispanics are lazy, you just can't trust Blacks, folks with Polish ancestry are stupid, Catholics are idol worshippers, the Church of Jesus Christ of Latter Day Saints is a cult, all Middle Eastern people are dangerous, the inhabitants of Kentucky are all inbred idiots, all men with long hair smoke pot, tattoos are a sign of the devil, all New Yorkers are inconsiderate, pushy bastards, Nebraskans are all just dumb farmers, the Orientals are taking over the US, all Jewish folks are greedy, money-hungry tightwads, and on and on and on and.... Yucky programming (according to my programming, obviously...)!

As a result, we fear (or are afraid of what they will or won't do) Hispanics, Blacks, Polish folks, Catholics, etc. We also have learned to fear such diverse things as failure, success, being alone, crowds, commitment, lack of commitment, death, life, heights, holes in the ground, not being liked, the future, dentists, flying, driving, walking, running, our government, other governments and a whole slew of other things probably including being afraid that other folks may think we're afraid of something. Whew!

So what can we do about it! The first choice is obviously "nothing". We can just continue through life being afraid of whatever it is we're afraid of. Or – we can at least sort of understand how we started being afraid of this stuff in the first place and redirect this fear energy to doing something – anything – that will help us blast through this roadblock to fun living. If we are able to honestly recognize that we indeed do have a fear (and we do) and want to get over it (it's not a requirement but it could be a good thing), then it will probably be easier if we can get some help with our little project. A helper – maybe professional help if we're trying to address a life-limiting fear – will make the whole process easier. About the only way I know of to conquer a fear (or use it to our advantage to learn something) is to meet it – or even greet it – face to face.

To overcome the fear of heights for example, we just need to have the experience of being in places that are "high". It might work out best to start low and work our way to high. Or maybe not. Take your pick. With a helper to encourage us – or maybe even hold us – we could walk to the edge of the second level of a parking garage and look down. Then the third level, then…OK, you get the idea. It won't be long until we get reprogrammed, change the fear to excited enthusiasm and perch on the edge of the Grand Canyon to enjoy the sunrise. Cool!

To overcome a fear of public speaking, we need to speak in public. To overcome a fear of flying, we need to fly more. Pretty simple, huh? Yeah, right! Just taking the first step is a major obstacle to all of us. That's why a helper is a pretty good idea. Helpers and research coupled with open-minded thinking – can also help us with our fears of, misconceptions of, and prejudices against – concepts or people. Yes, we will always have the right to hold our own opinions so this doesn't mean that we have to "buy in" to the beliefs or values of others. But if we are able to understand how we have become programmed in our thinking and beliefs over the years, it's a bunch easier to understand how the same thing happens to everyone else on the face of the earth. We gain an appreciation of others' beliefs and ways of living and with our restructured thinking, grant them the "right" to live their lives any way they see fit (within generally accepted parameters – which might not be all that great either come to think of it).

One last thing. Overcoming one fear helps to develop a personal mental process and a feeling of success that can help us address the next one. The more we work on this, the easier it becomes. Even though it may sound a little strange, a few of us sometimes start to get such a surge out of conquering fears that we actually start to look for new exciting, adrenaline-pumping adventures. Now, that is scary!

Our fears provide a great opportunity to learn more about ourselves and the world we live in. That's probably worth doing. I think I'll go find a high place. I really need to work on that...

More Scary Stuff

With the probable exception of some basic instincts – or motivation toward self-preservation – we've just flat *learned* to be afraid of about all the rest of the stuff we're afraid of. I know, the word "about" is a cop-out but I'm using it because I'm not really sure where this next mega-fear comes from.

The one fear that trips most of us up is – the FEAR of the UNKNOWN!! It has provided the foundation for some really great movies and TV programs, but it has also managed to slap the snot out of most of us at one time or another. If someone will hum the theme to "The Twilight Zone", I'll proceed. Thank you.

To start, let's lump a bunch of this together into the category we'll simply label as "The Future" (I think I'm overdoing this capitalization stuff. Sorry...) Most of us have a tendency to spend an inordinate amount of time and energy thinking about what is lurking just around the corner. We imagine (as in image – create a mental picture of) all sorts of bad things. We latch onto a few perceived facts and using our worst mental programming, fill in the blanks with the very worst negative scenarios we can possibly conjure up. We then extrapolate from this erroneous foundation through all the imaginary conversations and situations to the most creative, catastrophic conclusion possible. What a cool thing to be able to do! But here's the best part. If we focus really, really hard on our mental movie, there's a fairly good chance that some of it may actually come true!

For those of you who are sure that I've blown a gasket, just hangy on a minute and you'll see where I'm going with this...

OK, back to the future (I think I'll suggest that as a title for a movie trilogy...). Here's what we know for sure about our future. Nothing! Zip! Nada! Gar Nichts! Zero! It just ain't happened yet – at least that we know of. And yes, based on our knowledge of the <u>facts</u> related to a given situation coupled with a fair amount of deductive reasoning, we can predict with varying degrees of accuracy what **may** happen on down the road. But can we really know? Ain't no way! Life has altogether too many variables to be able to plug them into a pat formula to predict the future.

I could waste time and space here giving you a pile of examples on how our personal projections have turned out to be something other than we expected. We've all had enough life experiences so we can individually look back and grab a few dozen on our own. Just think about projected conversations or confrontations with your boss, employees, significant other or children that never came to pass and you'll get the idea.

We "what if" and "yeah but" ourselves into inaction and/or mega-stress. We numb ourselves out to prevent us from facing our imaginary future. We think of a thousand ways to avoid the catastrophic future that we're so certain awaits us. Why do we do that?

What's the alternative to this miserable approach to life? How about taking whatever facts – I repeat, facts – we can gather on the situation and, using them as a foundation for our projections, fill in the blanks (the unknown stuff) with <u>positive</u> scenarios. For planning purposes and to provide a bit of flexibility, it's a decent idea to snag maybe two or three different <u>positive</u> possible blank fillers that could provide a couple of <u>positive</u> outcomes. Then, focus on these positives and start taking whatever steps you need to take to address your situation. Slide into your future with the probable assurance that the outcome will – at least in the long run – be beneficial to everyone concerned. If the outcome is not nearly as pleasant as you would have wanted, at least look for the lesson contained in the whole situation. There probably is one in there for you.

Focusing on the potential positives really does give us a distinct advantage. It first of all, provides a more constructive (as opposed to self-destructive) foundation to use to draw up a reasonably logical plan of action. It helps us feel better about the whole process. Instead of being scared about the possible monsters lurking in the darkness somewhere down our path, we are better able to use our adrenaline surges as the fuel to blast us into – and through – the upcoming adventure. And – no BS here – the more we focus on positive efforts and a resulting positive outcome to our situation, the more likely it is that the end result of our endeavor really will be **positive**! It's sort of like a self-fulfilling prophecy thing. We will usually get out of life no more than we expect.

Our mind is pretty incredible. It is capable of whisking us down the road to our own special hell – or propelling us toward a considerably more desirable destination. The direction we wind up traveling is up to us.

Lessons from Geese

Fact 1: As each goose flaps its wings, it creates an "uplift" for the birds that follow. By flying in a "V" formation, the whole flock adds 71% greater flying range than if each bird flew alone.

Lesson: People who share a common direction and sense of community can get where they are going quicker and easier because they are traveling on the thrust of one another.

Fact 2: When a goose falls out of formation, it suddenly feels the drag and resistance of flying alone. It quickly moves back into formation to take advantage of the lifting power of the bird in front of it.

Lesson: If we have as much common sense as a goose, we stay in formation with those headed where we want to go. We are willing to accept their help and give our help to others.

Fact 3: When the lead goose tires, it rotates back into the formation and another goose flies to the point position.

Lesson: It pays to take turns doing the hard tasks and sharing leadership. As with geese, people are interdependent on each others' skills, capabilities, and unique arrangements of gifts, talents, or resources.

Fact 4: Geese flying in formation honk to encourage those up front to keep up their speed.

Lesson: We need to make sure our honking is encouraging. In groups where there is encouragement, the production is much greater. The power of encouragement (to stand by one's heart or core values and encourage the heart and core of others) is the quality of honking we seek.

Fact 5: When a goose gets sick, wounded, or shot down, two geese drop out of formation and follow it down to help protect it. They stay with it until it dies or is able to fly again. Then, they launch out with another formation or catch up with the flock.

Lesson: If we have as much sense as geese, we will stand by each other in difficult times as well as when we are strong.

Author Unknown

Mirrors...

Mirrors, mirrors all around,
Why don't I hear the joyful sound
Of myself clapping as I stroll by?
Is it you or is it I?

Aarghhh! My sincere apologies to the real poets of the world! The things I do to amuse myself...

Mirrors lie. All those pieces of glass with the reflective coating on the back – lie. You know they do. They never, never give us a true picture of ourselves. First of all of course, everything we see in them is backwards. We don't see "us". We see a skewed, backwards "us". It's not at all what other people see. We also frequently see ourselves as too fat, too skinny, too tall, too short, too old, too young, too wrinkled, nose too big, nose too small...

Any of the perceptions that I just mentioned could be a realistic interpretation of our reflection – or they may be in reality, totally inaccurate. We may feel the need to diet, diet, diet because we see ourselves as much too fat when in reality, we're about twenty pounds underweight. We may see giant wrinkles under our eyes and make a panic call to our friendly reconstructive surgeon when in reality, it would take a magnifying glass to positively identify the tiniest of creases. And I'm not really a wrinkled, graying, fuzzy, balding, old geezer. The mirror is clearly showing me as a mature gentleman with interesting, distinguishing features.

Unless we're putting out a bunch of effort to really see that which is being reflected back to us, we are only going to see that which we expect to see. Even then we'll never hit 100 percent accuracy. It's just the way our little minds work.

Our self-image, even without a mirror, is always at least a few degrees off from reality. We may imagine (image) ourselves as charming, outgoing and friendly when in reality, we may be a loud, obnoxious pain in the rear. Or we may view ourselves as lower than pond scum and not deserving of a second look from anyone when in reality, we may be quite nice and pleasant to be around. It would be beneficial if we could have a more realistic picture of ourselves. It would be good if we could be more aware of our strengths – and of course, it would be really good if we could identify some of the areas that could use a bit of improvement.

Here's where other folks can come in handy. First, another's honest evaluation of us has the potential of providing at least a basic view of ourselves. You gotta remember what's liable to happen here, though. To begin with, the "honest" part of the evaluation may (will?) be questionable. Well-meaning people sometimes just flat lie to keep from hurting our feelings. Apart from that, their observations of us <u>will</u> be shaded by <u>their</u> experiences (programming). We will be the recipient of their perception of us. And to top it all off, we will hear and process their information according to our experiences and programming. This may or may not correlate with their intended meaning. About the best we can hope for here is that we may get an indication of how we are perceived by others. Or use the old rule of thumb. (OK – so it's my thumb and my rule...) If one person out of a hundred thinks you are a doofus, you probably don't need to worry about it. Get up to fifty people and you likely have a problem to address. If ninety-nine percent of your acquaintances agree that you're a butthead, you can expect to receive your certification in the mail sometime next week.

The remainder of this equation for performing a self-check using other people requires using our own self-evaluation abilities – which are of course, packaged in our own personal box of brightly-colored perceptions. (Are you getting the idea that none of this stuff will work out perfectly?) It boils down to a saying I heard a long time ago. If you point your finger –

accusingly or in judgment – toward another person, you will always have three fingers pointing right back at yourself.

This is the mirror we alluded to at the beginning of this chapter. We see and subsequently condemn or judge in others, the imperfections or short-comings that exist in some form within ourselves. Our observations of others and our resulting comments – or even thoughts – can give us a good idea of some of the things it might be beneficial for us to work on.

Here are a couple of examples. The words "He's an idiot!" from our lips is an indication that we may feel inadequate, stupid or an "idiot" relative to some section of our lives. "She dresses like a pig!" may mean that we're not at all happy about some part of our appearance – or the impression we feel we're giving to others. The flip side of this is that the positive thoughts we have about others, whether they are expressed verbally or not, often reflect the positive qualities that exist within ourselves. There is no pat formula for determining the meaning of these comments or thoughts. They can only be interpreted by their owner. That would be us.

None of life's mirrors can provide a completely accurate reflection. But they can at least give us a few hints of some things we might want to think about.

Grandpa's Wisdom

Don't name a pig you plan to eat.

Country fences need to be horse high, pig tight and bull strong.

Life is not about how fast you run, or how high you climb, but how well you bounce.

Keep skunks and bankers at a distance.

Life is simpler when you plow around the stumps.

Mortgaging a future crop is saddling a wobbly colt.

A bumblebee is faster than a John Deere tractor.

Trouble with a milk cow is she won't stay milked.

Don't skinny dip with snapping turtles.

Words that soak into your ears are whispered, not yelled.

Meanness don't happen overnight.

To know how country folks are doing, look at their barns, not their houses.

Never lay an angry hand on a kid or an animal, it just ain't helpful.

Teachers, bankers, and hoot owls sleep with one eye open.

Forgive your enemies. It messes with their heads.

Don't sell your mule to buy a plow.

Two can live as cheap as one if one don't eat.

Don't corner something meaner than you.

It don't take a very big person to carry a grudge.

Don't go huntin' with a fellow named Chug-A-Lug.

You can't unsay a cruel thing.

Every path has some puddles.

When you wallow with pigs, expect to get dirty.

The best sermons are lived, not preached.

Most of the stuff people worry about happening, don't.

Lazy and Quarrelsome are ugly sisters.

The Sky is Falling...

Yuck! It's all yuck! The sky is falling, the earth is splitting apart, a giant asteroid is headed our way and we're all going to hell! Don't believe me? Just check today's headlines or catch the six o'clock news. We're slogging our way through the cesspool of existence. We're all just residue tumbling our way through life's sewer to the Great Waste Plant in the Sky. Yuck!

Now we all know that life is honestly not all that bad. Even though some of us are traveling a pretty rough road not necessarily by our own choosing, many of us are enjoying a whole slew of life's good things. But we all are being bombarded by negatives from the media, TV, music, coworkers, acquaintances, family and unfortunately even ourselves from time to time. For those of us who aren't too thrilled with our lot in life, these negatives can have the effect of reinforcing our foundation perception that "life sucks".

There probably has been the equivalent of a giant library of books and articles written related to the power of thinking positively and the excellent effects of positive imaging and positive attitudes. Many of us have benefited immensely from the concepts presented in these materials and all of the videos and tapes that reinforce this type of thinking. If you haven't yet looked into any of these resources, I'm suggesting that it might be advantageous for you to do so. Here's why.

Basically, we have become programmed through our experiences and various sensory inputs, to be what we are now with our individual beliefs, hang-ups and approaches to life. Even if you're not too sure about the "programming" concept, there is little doubt that we are all heavily influenced by our environment as good or as bad as it may be (or may have been). Our environment will continue to influence our thoughts, attitudes and subsequent actions to some degree until the day we die. The major question here is – would we prefer to go through the remainder of our lives downtrodden, dejected, depressed, uncomfortable and continually looking at the down side of life …or would we prefer to be happier and be able to enjoy our stroll along life's pathway? Most of us, without hesitation, would choose the latter.

If you'd like to give it a try, here are a few suggestions to help get you started. First, ELIMINATE, STAY AWAY FROM, AVOID, IGNORE, DISREGARD and STOP ABSORBING THE NEGATIVE CRAP! Second, actively look for the positives in life, set some achievable goals related to the other areas you'd like to improve and start taking the steps to get there.

As a beginning point, you might start by writing down a list of the good things in your life. It's a "gratitude check" and with just a little thought, you should be able to come up with a pretty decent list. Start with the fact that you woke up this morning and go from there. Add to your list as you go along. (Nature is always a good source for cool stuff for the list.) Keep your list handy because I can about guarantee that every once in a while, things will turn to yuck and you'll need a boost.

If the "news" is getting you down, just stop watching it on TV and/or stop reading the paper or news magazines. It's OK to be informed, however if you can feel (Oh dear, isn't that terrible..!) the emotions associated with the natural disasters, killings, car crashes, abductions, terrorist acts, etc., that likely means you're absorbing this negative information and slamming it right into your subconscious. Not a particularly great thing to do.

If the other TV programs you watch – or the radio programs you listen to – focus on conflicts or the hardships of life, you might be better off switching channels. If you listen to "woe is me" music, try to find something more upbeat or more relaxing. Or just turn the TV or radio off altogether. Take some time to think about some really cool stuff. Yes, short visits to fantasyland are permissible. Be careful if you're driving though and remember that sometime you'll need to revert back to reality. (Dang…)

If the people you're normally around tend to be negative (bitchy, whiney, grouchy, complaining), try to find somebody more positive to hang out with. Yes, I understand that sometimes we're forced to work with these folks, but try to limit your exposure to them as much as possible. And yes, I also realize that we're living with some of them, too. Just do what you can to improve the environment (check first to see if there are some changes you need to make within yourself) and if that doesn't work out well, you may need to take further action later. Oh, by the way, yelling and shouting – especially in anger – is a GIANT negative reinforcer. Just stop doing it…

If you're a true beginner with this positive stuff, here's a sort of a silly place to start. When someone asks "How ya doin'?", stop answering "crappy" or "not too bad". Try using "Good, thanks – and you?" Or maybe "Just fine, thank you". (You can transition to "Super!!" later on down the road.) This technique may seem a little strange to you, however it honestly does help your mind accept the positive reinforcements you're trying to feed it. One caution here. If you're stuck in a sucky situation and not taking steps to improve it, you're really not "good" or "fine" much less "Super". You're just stuck and doin' kind of crappy. You need to do something – take some action – to try to better your circumstance so there is a reasonable level of honesty in your "good" answer.

One last thought here. Positive thinking and positive attitudes promote positive results. True, the immediate results may not be exactly what you had visualized; they may even be somewhat uncomfortable. Generally though, they will be beneficial and will likely be a good step toward a personal, positive result. I firmly believe that we are here in this life to learn and that life is filled with lessons. So as part of the positive thinking process, take time to look for the lessons especially in those situations that are uncomfortable. And try to SMILE more! At the very least, it will make people wonder what the heck you've been up to….

HOW TO STAY YOUNG

1. Throw out nonessential numbers. This includes age, weight and height. Let the doctor worry about them. That is why you pay him/her.

2. Keep only cheerful friends. The grouches pull you down.

3. Keep learning. Learn more about the computer, crafts, gardening, whatever. Never let the brain idle. "An idle mind is the devil's workshop," - and the devil's name is Alzheimer's.

4. Enjoy the simple things.

5. Laugh often, long and loud. Laugh until you gasp for breath.

6. The tears happen. Endure, grieve, and move on. The only person who is with us our entire life is ourselves. Be ALIVE while you are alive.

7. Surround yourself with what you love, whether it's family, pets, keepsakes, music, plants, hobbies, whatever. Your home is your refuge.

8. Cherish your health: If it is good, preserve it. If it is unstable, improve it. If it is beyond what you can improve, get help.

9. Don't take guilt trips. Take a trip to the mall, to the next county, to a foreign country, but NOT to where the guilt is.

10. Tell the people you love that you love them, at every opportunity.

AND ALWAYS REMEMBER:
Life is not measured by the number of breaths we take, but by the moments that take our breath away.

I'd Rather Live in Fantasyland...

OK, it's time for a .... REALITY CHECK!! Don't you just hate it when that happens? Here we are minding our own business and dividing our time between Denialville and Fantasyland – and I come along and start to get pushy about this reality stuff. I know. I am really inconsiderate.

So why am I bringing this up and completely disrupting your life's flow? Because I'm basically a stinker who likes to stir things up just to see if I can get a couple of crawdads to crawl to the top of the lobster tank. They're easier to fish out and dispose of that way.

Here's the first little critter you might want to check for. It's probably labeled "Not My Fault" – or something like that. This one shows up to the strains of "The Whiner's Lullaby", "The Complainer's Serenade" or the "I'm a Victim – You're a Victim So We Have a Right to Feel Really, Really Bad" choral arrangement...plus other tunes too numerous to mention.

Many of us put a lot of effort into avoiding taking any personal responsibility for our lives and refusing to be accountable for our present situation. We lay the blame squarely on our parents, teachers, bosses, family members, bad guys and anyone else we can think of that might fit the bill. Why? Because this looks like the easy way out. By laying the blame on someone else, we escape the pain of reality – and the discomfort and work of having to do something ourselves to improve the situation. It's our personal little cop-out that could keep us in our rut until the day we die.

About the only way I know of to get rid of this little guy is to modify our thinking patterns (do some mental reprogramming) so we can face reality and accept the fact that each one of us is ultimately accountable for where we are in our lives. Extreme circumstances aside, we all have the ability – perhaps with some outside help – to make some positive changes in our lives. The first step here is to honestly recognize that we personally are responsible for where we are in life. There may have been strong outside influences but we ultimately made the decision to do what we're doing. Remember, no one can <u>control</u> our lives unless we give them permission to do so. We always have options. Important note: If you are being controlled under threats of physical or emotional harm – GET HELP NOW! One of the universal rules of life is that nothing is likely to change until we personally do something – until we take action to improve those things we want to improve.

That brings me to the second critter which we'll label "Denial". This can take many forms. "Things aren't really all that bad." "I'm really not codependent." "I don't care what Gene says, I'm really not responsible for my present situation." "I'm not addicted to anything." "I'm not always sleeping or on the computer because I'm trying to hide from my life." "I won't do anything because I know sooner or later that things will get better." "Not my fault." Plus a few hundred other similar excuses (rationalizations to keep us from facing reality).

We are sooo proficient at rationalizing our way into inaction. Just comes with a lot of practice I guess. Maybe we would be slightly better off if we started practicing admitting our mistakes or errors in judgment. Geez folks, we all screw up. We all make emotional, spur-of-the-moment decisions. We all make projections using half-truths or skewed facts. Our decisions frequently do not provide the results we expected. So what! Unless we're dead, we can always learn from our experiences and our mistakes – and we can try to do it better or differently next time.

Just for the heck of it, here are a few simple examples of screw-ups (rationalizations) and what we could do about them. "I was late to work because I had to stop to get gas." Fueling up the night before or getting up earlier could prevent that. "I was late to a meeting because I couldn't find the car keys." Get into the habit of always hanging them on a hook or putting them in a certain spot. "My electricity was turned off because I forgot to pay the bill." Set up a budget and stick to it – and always keep your bills together so you can find them easily. "My car engine overheated and "froze" up." Check the coolant and oil level periodically. "I got fired because my boss had it out for me." Calling him a butthead probably didn't help either. "My 'old lady' kicked me out of the house on my rear." Think it might have had something to do with the two chicks you've been shacking up with? "My pile of bills just keeps getting bigger and bigger." Back to the budget – and either spend less or make more money. You get the idea.

And yes, sometimes stuff happens that puts our world in a tail-spin. Illness, deaths in the family, depressed economy, business failures, natural disasters, etc., can all negatively impact our lives. These things are pretty much beyond our control. The best we can do when significant events occur is to stay flexible, develop a plan of action and keep on truckin'. It is when the major events happen that the basics become even more important. It won't help one little bit to waste our time whining, complaining or grouching about our misfortune. Now it is doubly important to honestly evaluate our situation, accept reality and do the things we need to do to move on down the road.

Reality can sometimes be pretty sucky. It is all up to us to individually recognize (face) our personal reality, accept responsibility for the portion of it that belongs to us and do the things we need to do to try to make it better.

GREAT TRUTHS THAT LITTLE CHILDREN HAVE LEARNED

No matter how hard you try, you can't baptize cats.

When your Mom is mad at your Dad, don't let her brush your hair.

If your sister hits you, don't hit her back. They always catch the second person.

Never ask your 3-year old brother to hold a tomato.

You can't trust dogs to watch your food.

Don't sneeze when someone is cutting your hair.

Never hold a Dust-Buster and a cat at the same time.

You can't hide a piece of broccoli in a glass of milk.

Don't wear polka-dot underwear under white shorts.

Puppies still have bad breath even after eating a tic tac.

School lunches stick to the wall.

The best place to be when you're sad is Grandpa's lap.

What Once Was...Ain't No More...

The above chapter title has been created intentionally to annoy the English teachers of the world – and come to think of it, everyone else who insists that it is an absolute sin against Mankind to use anything less than "proper, acceptable" English – ever. Having said that and subsequently feeling much better about life in general (it never takes much to perk me up...), I'd also like to express my sincere appreciation to all you folks who have somehow managed to keep our English (or American, if you will) language from completely deteriorating into one giant heap of linguistic compost. Of course, that will never prevent me from tossing rotting potato peelings on the pile from time to time.

Where were we? Oh, yes – what once was... Rather than beat around the bush and try to lead into this in a semi-logical manner, I'll get right to the point. The past is **gone** – vanished, disappeared in a cloud of dust and a hearty "Hi, Ho Silver!" It is history, not real, mental vapor, and gone, gone, gone!

"Yabutt..."

"Yabutt" nothing. The past is gone! OK, I do understand that a bunch of stuff has happened before now to influence what "now" is. And sometimes it's good to take a look at the past to see just how the heck we got to our "now". With a little luck, the record of the past will not have been so over-skewed by our individual and collective perceptions that we will be limited in our ability to make current rational decisions.

Well, so much for luck! We do change the past, don't we? We remember what we think we remember, then we shade it slightly with our current situation or viewpoint of life and the events surrounding us (is this a reprogramming thing?) – and remember the past as we think it should be remembered. The really good things that have happened just keep getting better and better. Unfortunately, the bad things have a tendency to get worse and worse.

Since I'm into "positives" - even exaggerated ones - I'm going to give myself permission to remember the good stuff in any absolutely wonderful way I want. Shucks, I may even extrapolate a bit and push some of these fantastic memories right into Fantasyland – for just a few minutes, that is. Then I'll come back to reality…maybe…

As far as the bad stuff is concerned – well, I think I'll handle those a bit differently. Let's see now…bad stuff…hmmm, I can't remember anything particularly bad. Oh wait, there was that time I…no, that wasn't all that bad… Ok, how about the time…no, that wasn't actually bad…

What I do remember though, are a bunch of times that were darned uncomfortable! Times that I used poor information and/or logic to reach a decision – or times that I had to do things that I really didn't want to do (commonly because I had done something goofy previously to put me in an uncomfortable situation). Or times that I might have acted too impulsively – or even the times that something happened that was out of my control (a sh-- happens thing). Nah, I can't remember all the details of this stuff. I just have a general recollection of the events – and of some of the things I did to rectify the situation or changes I made in the way I was thinking and conducting my life.

Get the idea? Of course you do. Too many of us have a tendency to live in the past. We remember events and situations as "bad". Our minds automatically fill in the missing details with exaggerated "facts". We relive those bad moments complete with every associated emotion we can conjure up. We are sad, depressed and sometimes flat miserable. We resort to medications (and other readily available related alternatives) to relieve the pain. Life just sucks!

The past is not real, folks! It is gone! The only way it becomes "real" is by allowing our minds to push it into the forefront of our thoughts. What has happened – has happened. We can't change it even though at times we may desperately want to. The only reality is **now**! Our past has brought us here – to our "now". "Now" is the only time we can do stuff – not yesterday, not tomorrow –only now.

You might think about using some of your "now" to put the past to rest. Look for the lessons those uncomfortable events might hold for you. What can you learn from those situations that will help make your life easier on down the road? Turning "bad" events into lessons will help move them further back in the mental file cabinet. Apologies where appropriate and forgiveness of both yourself and others as necessary can be a couple of other useful tools to diminish the impact and the nagging of the memories of the past. Handing the negative memories over to your personal spiritual "leader" is often useful. (You'll probably still need to do something in addition though.) Also, focusing on the positives of the past will help to lessen the impact of the negatives.

If your "now" is pretty sucky, all you can do is deal with it the best way you know how. If you can find an immediate lesson in the situation – great! If you don't see one, you may have to wait for a later "now" when you can see a bit more clearly. Life's like that. Just remember that it won't be long until this "now" is gone. I think that's one of those "This too shall pass" things.

The past? Remember the cool stuff and as for the rest of the garbage – LET IT GO!!!

GREAT TRUTHS THAT ADULTS HAVE LEARNED

Raising teenagers is like nailing Jell-O to a tree.

Wrinkles don't hurt.

Families are like fudge...mostly sweet, with a few nuts.

The best way to keep kids at home is to make the home a pleasant atmosphere and let the air out of their tires.

Today's mighty oak is just yesterday's nut that held its ground.

Laughing is good exercise. It's like jogging on the inside.

Middle age is when you choose your cereal for the fiber, not the toy.

If you can remain calm, you just don't have all the facts.

Eat a live toad first thing in the morning, and nothing worse can happen to you the rest of the day!

Life's golden age is when the kids are too old to need baby-sitters and too young to borrow the family car.

Really rich people are much more likely to drown in yacht accidents.

Mechanics' cars break down too.

THE RULES FOR BEING HUMAN

1. You will receive a body. You may like it or hate it, but it will be yours for the entire period this time around.

2. You will learn lessons. You are enrolled in a full-time, informal school called life. Each day you will have the opportunity to learn lessons. You may like the lessons or think them irrelevant and stupid.

3. There are no mistakes - only lessons. Growth is a process of trial and error and experimentation. The "failed" experiments are as much a part of the process as the experiment that ultimately "works".

4. A lesson is repeated until it is learned. A lesson will be presented to you in various forms until you have learned it. When you have learned it, then you can go on to the next lesson.

5. Learning lessons does not end. There is no part of life that does not contain its lessons. If you are alive, there are lessons to be learned.

6. There is no better there than here. When your "there" has become a "here", you will simply obtain another "there" that will again, look better than "here".

7. Others are merely mirrors of you. You cannot love or hate something about another person unless it reflects to you something you love or hate about yourself.

8. What you make of your life is up to you. You have all the tools and resources you need. What you do with them is up to you. The choice is yours.

9. The answers lie inside you. The answers to life's questions lie inside you. All you need do is ask, look, listen and trust.

10. You will forget all this. You will forget all of these rules unless you constantly work to stay in the "present". Your ego will try to trick you into living in your past or fantasizing about your future. By doing either of these, you lose contact with the "present" and become asleep to the possibilities of life.

Unknown

Why me?

Thunder, lightening, snow, sleet, hail, plague, pestilence and gloom of night. Oh yeah – locusts and frogs, too.

Some folks just seem to always be on the receiving end of life's manure spreader. And I don't mean this as one of those personal perception things either. It's not like these good people are just whining and moaning about their sad situation. They really are getting hit with what seems to be more than their fair share of yucky stuff. I wonder why that is?

Do you think it's possible that in some instances, this might have something to do with "Life's Lessons"? Remember the "Rules for Being Human" chapter? You might want to look at it again because from what I've seen, there's probably more truth in it than many of us would like to admit. These are the four items I'm thinking about in particular:

2. You will learn lessons. You are enrolled in a full-time, informal school called life. Each day you will have the opportunity to learn lessons. You may like the lessons or think them irrelevant and stupid.
3. There are no mistakes - only lessons. Growth is a process of trial and error and experimentation. The "failed" experiments are as much a part of the process as the experiment that ultimately "works".
4. A lesson is repeated until it is learned. A lesson will be presented to you in various forms until you have learned it. When you have learned it, then you can go on to the next lesson.
5. Learning lessons does not end. There is no part of life that does not contain its lessons. If you are alive, there are lessons to be learned.

I've come to believe that one of the reasons we're here on this earth is to learn stuff. And, I think it's very possible that old number 4 is pretty much on the mark. Yeah, I know. Some of you, based on your life experiences and mental programming, will think that old Gene's way off base here. That's OK. But what if there is an element of truth in this? Isn't it worth checking into further – especially if we're the one who's on the receiving end of all the junk? It would seem to me that if there's *anything* we could do to make our lives a little easier and more enjoyable, we oughtta at least give it a try.

Just as a suggestion – especially if you are the "dumpee" – why not take some time to look at the uncomfortable events in your life to see if there's something you might be able to learn from them. Like what? Oh, like focusing more on the positive aspects of life, learning to be more caring and considerate of others, making life changes to lift yourself out of your rut, modifying your thinking from just survival (even though this may be a critical issue for you right now) to what you would really enjoy accomplishing in life, acquiring more patience (I'm still working on this), shedding some of your fears of the future and the unknown, focusing more on the "now" and less on the past, making amends for past misdeeds, learning to be happy with who and what you are (not necessarily satisfied) – and other stuff like that.

The possibilities for learning are unlimited. And because we are who we are, my potential lessons are different than yours. The neat thing about it though, is that if we spend just a little time thinking about this stuff, we'll know. Sooner or later, we'll know what we need to learn or change in our lives. In my opinion, sooner is better. The sooner I can learn from my experiences, the sooner they will be history and I won't have to keep going through the same type of yucky goo.

Let me flip back to the "positive approach to life" for just a minute. Positive expectations can help bring about positive changes in our lives. No, I'm not saying that viewing our world through rose colored glasses is in the least bit beneficial. I'm saying that if we'll take a realistic look at our situation and take the time to plan and take action to improve that situation, there's a very good chance that beneficial changes *will* occur which will result in a positive outcome overall. I always need to toss in that danged "overall" because sometimes the immediate results of our efforts are quite uncomfortable and it's difficult to view those as being the least little bit positive. But from what I've seen (and experienced), these uncomfortable moments help provide the greatest opportunity for learning – and that will give us the insights we need to move closer to our "positive" destination.

One more thing along this line. Our focus – the stuff we think about a lot – will generally be one of the main engines that powers us through life. That's pretty obvious, huh? But have you noticed what happens when we over-focus on something? We wind up expending so much time and energy on that one thing that we miss a bunch of the other really cool stuff. For example, do you know of anyone who seems to spend an inordinate amount of time in the doctor's office or at the emergency room? With exceptions of course, many of these folks have just developed a super-focus on their bodies and all the ways it can malfunction. I haven't researched this, but this just might be another example of the 80 – 20 rule. Twenty per-cent of the people make up eighty percent of the doctor's office and hospital business. It could be because they've over-focused on this area of their lives.

There are other folks who, consciously or not, are focused on a particular fear. They'll probably have a tendency to do a whole bunch of things to overprotect themselves from having to experience that situation or event. Yet, through the efforts they exert, they may well put themselves in a position where they are forced to face at least a related fear. Life's strange like that. There's probably a lesson in there somewhere.

As just another suggestion then, maybe we would be better off to focus mostly on the good stuff – the good things around us and the good things we would like to experience in our lives. Who knows. We may just get what we're thinking about!

SUCCESS

At age 4 success is… not peeing in your pants.

At age 12 success is… having friends.

At age 16 success is… having a driver's license.

At age 20 success is… going all the way.

At age 35 success is… having money.

At age 50 success is… having money.

At age 60 success is… going all the way.

At age 70 success is… having a driver's license.

At age 75 success is… having friends.

At age 80 success is… not peeing in your pants

The "G" Word...

OK – so there are lots of "G" words, however for now we'll focus on one particular word that has created (I would have used the word "wreaked", but I personally think it's a silly word that always seems to have an umbilical connection to the word "havoc") a bunch of havoc and confusion in our lives – and has been responsible for severely damping our ability to really enjoy life. The word?

GUILT!

Here's Gene's definition...Guilt: Our personal ability to feel badly about something that did or did not happen – and to punish ourselves accordingly for the dastardly deed(s). We are cads, inconsiderate slobs, unthinking bastards, inattentive morons, uncaring imbeciles to be forever damned to a self-imposed sentence of remorse and mental anguish! If that won't take the fun out of a hog-calling contest, I don't know what will.

So where's all this guilt coming from? Maybe Mom? She's always been an expert at laying the guilt trip on us. How about our spouse or significant other? Oh man, forget one little ol' anniversary and we're toast forever. Maybe from our children? "We never played catch in the back yard and that's why I took drugs and went to prison!" "You always liked Petey best!" "You kicked me out of the house when I was only 37 and because of that, I can never buy a new car!" Or maybe we managed to do something really stupid that got ourselves – and other people in a heap of trouble.

What's the common thread in all of these situations – and in every other guilt-related event that we could ever think of? These incidents all happened in the **past**! OK – maybe that's not much of a revelation, but it's the primary factor in our feelings (anguish, remorse, etc.) that we keep ignoring. The past is gone, done, history, bye-bye, hasta luego, and kaput! Unfortunately, we have a tendency to exert entirely too much effort dragging an event from the past back into our wee little brains where we can examine it under a microscope to reinforce once again, how absolutely dumb and unthoughtful we've been. Sometimes we'll even go to the trouble to contemplate a future situation and decide on a course of action based on how guilty we may or may not feel depending on our actions. Eeeeewwww!

From here, it looks like we need to take care of a couple of things. First, we need to get rid of all the guilt crap that's piled up in our heads. And second, we need to keep from throwing any more crap on the pile. Hmmm, only two things. We can handle that.

I'm pretty sure that at this point, we all honestly know where our guilt is coming from. Yep – from right inside our devious little minds. It's all a personal response to a given situation. A response that depends almost entirely on our past experiences – and, yep again, our mental/emotional programming. So let's take a look at our guilt generator to see if there are a couple of switches we can flip.

First – the past. We can't change it so we'll just have to deal with it – either by taking action to rectify a situation (if appropriate) or by changing the way we're thinking about it. Sometimes, we really do need to <u>do</u> something. If we've called our best friend an butt-head and are now feeling guilty about it, we probably need to re-establish contact and make our apologies. What he or she then does with that apology is up to him/her, but at least we will have made a good effort to do the right thing. If our past actions have caused major, major problems for someone, we may need to put extra, extra effort into our attempts to rectify the situation.

The main thing here is <u>doing</u> something to make things better.

One word (OK – more than one) of caution. We probably shouldn't be doing "things" to make amends for our perceived transgressions strictly in an attempt to *make* others think better of us. It ain't agonna work. Even though we may desperately want other people to have a good opinion of us, what they think is completely beyond our control. Yes, we can influence the opinions of others, but we can never control it. And – it really is a waste of effort and emotion to even try. Too often, I think we may work for these approvals to try to reinforce or even build up our own feelings of self-worth. Pats on the back are nice and approval is good, however they are meaningful only when they are given spontaneously. Picture yourself trying really hard and doing everything you can possibly think of to snag some praise from a close friend. Picture yourself not getting one smidgeon of acclaim. Picture yourself getting royally ticked off at the stupidity of your friend. It can be a vicious, demoralizing cycle.

Doing "things" to rectify misunderstandings or hardships we may have imposed upon someone is logical and will likely be beneficial to everyone – ourselves included. And, once we've done what we think we need to do, we need to let it go! We have done all that we can do and no matter what the outcome is, it's over. Let's get on with life.

If we're feeling guilty about something that happened that we have no way in hell of ever doing anything to repair the situation, all we can do is let it go. Remember, the past is the past – and it's gone forever. All we can do is admit that we screwed up (if we really did), learn whatever it is we need to learn from our mistake and press on. We'll just try to do better from now on. Maybe we've already been doing better. Looks like good progress to me!

Now the future. Guilt very often, is the result of our granting others permission to control our thoughts, feelings and perhaps even our actions. No one can control us in any way without our consent. Folks, we have enough trouble controlling our own thoughts and emotions. It just doesn't make sense to grant anyone else the privilege of doing that. Flip the guilt consent switch to the "off" position. If this is a drastic change from your usual approach, you can about bet that sooner or later, somebody is going to be very unhappy. That's the chance we take. Of course, other folks have a right to feel any way they want about anything, don't they? It's beyond our control.

Guilt can be good in that it can give us an incentive to do things better. It can on the other hand, be really oppressive and can severely limit our ability to enjoy life and do those things we really want to do. All we can do is the best we can do. If we screw something up – and we will – we can learn from it and then do even better. Life's like that. Cool!

Busy, Busy, Busy.....

...busy, busy, busy, busy...busy, busy, bus... OK, slap me with a wet diaper! Enough of that silliness. Most of you know what I'm talking about though, right? That's us! Busy. Doing what? Stuff. What kinds of stuff? All kinds of stuff. Like what? You name it. Give me an example. Can't. Why not? Too busy...

OK – that's it! Blow the danged whistle! We need a Time Out!

Holy Smokes, Folks! We're going outta control. No, not all of us, of course. But there are enough of us pushing our physical, mental and emotional limits that it's worthwhile talking about it. Let me ask you this. When was the last time you just kicked back and looked at the clouds to see what cartoonish kinds of figures or shapes you could see in them? Or the last time you touched a plant leaf and really thought about how it felt and how amazing it was that it was an actual living thing? Or the last time you strolled leisurely down the road or path and thought about nothing in particular? Or the last time you watched a baby sleep and enjoyed the feeling of being a part of a great creation? Or the last time you leaned back in an easy chair and snoozed – not because you were completely worn out, but just because it seemed like a neat thing to do?

Many of us unfortunately, are the proud owners of the skewed assumption that we must always be doing something. OK, for those of you who have a tendency to get overly technical, we are *always* doing something – even when we're doing "nothing". You know what I mean. I'm referring to our obsession with physical and mental (and sometimes emotional) activity. We go to work, do stuff, talk with folks, go home, go to the store, go out to an activity, run errands, pay bills, haul the kids around, fix meals, do yard work, do house work, fix stuff, paint stuff, reorganize stuff, buy more stuff, watch TV, surf the web, and on and on. Even our vacations are so crammed with "doing" that we're pooped puppies by the time we get back home.

Yeah, I know. I have heard time and time again, "But I just have sooo much to do that I can't get it all done in a day!" There are probably several possible reasons for this comment. This person may be in a survival mode of operation with his/her day filled to overflowing with more than one job, caring for loved ones and trying to meet the demands of everyday living. Or this individual may just be a bit disorganized and have a difficult time establishing logical priorities. Or, maybe he/she isn't really all that busy but for some reason would like others to think he/she is. Or maybe this person has a difficult time saying "no" for a variety of reasons. Or perhaps this individual has become so accustomed to being busy or having some type of auditory input that to do otherwise is uncomfortable – again, for a variety of possible reasons.

We all have our individual, special reasons for being busy and admittedly, many of the reasons are completely valid. I'm suggesting however, that none of the reasons are valid enough. Every single one of us needs time to kick back for at least a few minutes each day to recharge our physical, mental and emotional batteries. And the busier we get, the more critical this recharge becomes.

Most of us know, or have known, people who have succumbed to the Go-Go-Go Syndrome. We have seen everything from burn-outs to complete physical, mental or emotional collapse. Suddenly, the go-go-go has turned into a stop-stop-stop. Everything that seemed to be such a high priority dropped dramatically in its ranking – probably closer to the level it should have been at in the first place.

I think it would be beneficial if we all made the small effort that it takes to reserve at least fifteen minutes a day just for us. Fifteen minutes for a time out to relax, meditate or just let the old brain cells cool down. Fifteen minutes to regroup and recharge our batteries. Just fifteen minutes. About one percent of our day. OK, considering all the other possible options, it might not be the absolute best fifteen minutes you've ever enjoyed in life but it's still worth doing. Give it a try. You'll like it…

I'm Gettin' Really Torqued!

For those of you who have been living in a cave for most of your lives, you can translate the "torqued" in the title of this chapter to "mad" or "angry". Actually, I was going to use a more descriptive word (which everyone understands) but I thought it would look tacky in bold print. I'd hate to tarnish my image, ya know.

However, for today's discussion of anger, let's quantify the intensity of our focus with the words "downright, PO'd!" I think that's quite clear. Let's proceed.

The first question is "What makes you really angry (as in PO'd)?"

Inconsiderate, rude people? Bad drivers? Lousy service? Brainless bosses? Dumb subordinates? Idiot lawyers? Answering machines? The government? Waiting in line? Foreigners? Big business? Potholes? Traffic jams? Airports? The news? TV programming? Your significant other? Your kids? Your neighbors? Uncle Harold? Aunt Edna? The stupid dog? The friggin' car? The damned washing machine? Your lost keys? The toilet? The pillow? Your socks?

Wanna know what makes me really, really mad?

Nothing...

Hmmm, OK – how about what sometimes makes me upset and sort of irritated?

That would be me.

Huh?

Me. Just me. I'm the one who "makes" me upset and sort of irritated once in a while. I'm the only one who can "make" me do that. No one else, no event, no situation can make me get mad. Our anger doesn't come from the outside. It can't. It's strictly an internal emotion that surges – and sometimes even erupts – as the result of our perception and feelings about an "outside" situation.

From the way it looks, we humans are probably designed and assembled with the brain wiring and foundation programming it takes to feel and express anger. Although experts disagree on the ability to logically differentiate between anger and distress in very young infants, we parents can all remember the early signals of displeasure to varying degrees in our youngin's. Spitting the strained peas in Grandma's face is a good example.

How did we learn how to be angry? From our exposure to anger around our humble abode and in the rest of our environment in our early years, we learned that getting hacked off is just what we humans do when we're not pleased with a given situation. We learned that it's OK – and sometimes even expected – that we make a yucky face, clench our fists, stomp our feet, beat on the table and scream obscenities at the top of our lungs (another strange expression that I suppose is not to be confused with using the middle or lower part of our lungs...our language is weird...). We learned – and duly programmed our subconscious – to react to the displeasing events in our lives with the appropriate (or for us personally – applicable) level and intensity of anger.

Guess what? It doesn't need to be like that. We all have the ability to reprogram our little minds to respond to the displeasing events in our lives in a less stressful and much quieter manner. No, it's not necessarily easy to do, however once we recognize and admit that our mega-anger is not something that is just normally a part of human nature – and that we *do* have the ability to consciously control it – we have completed a huge step in the right direction. Becoming hacked off is an automatic decision our minds make for us. Not becoming angry then, must be a conscious decision we make that will override our automatic one.

You might try this. The next time you feel the anger starting to surge, take just a couple of seconds – or a few minutes or longer - to realize what is happening, think briefly about the event or person who is triggering the anger, then decide if you really want to let your subconscious continue on it's programmed path – or if you want to consciously step in and modify this effort. Anger toward a person or situation can be expressed assertively – not aggressively - at a reasonable volume while being respectful of the rights and opinions of others. This *can* lead to open communications and a resolution of the problem. Will it? Who the hell knows but it's worth a shot. Sure beats the snot out of knocking somebody's skull in.

In the cooling-off period, you might just discover that the situation was not nearly as critical as you had first imagined. Perhaps someone (maybe you?) didn't have all the facts and the conflict was the just result of a misunderstanding. Maybe once you stand back and see the circumstances from a slightly different perspective, you might decide the whole thing was pretty silly to start with and there is nothing really worth pursuing. Or, you may even admit that entire situation was completely out of your control (influence) so getting angry is just a futile waste of energy.

Probably the worst thing anyone could do is suppress the anger. To tuck it away deep down inside. This could lead to major problems later either in a potential catastrophic confrontation, in a "torpedoing" of the other person – or in an eating away of your mental/emotional stability or deterioration of your physical being. Not a good thing to have happen.

Anger toward an object (car, refrigerator, keys) is pretty much a waste of effort and energy. It's likely a situation (damn car broke and I don't have the coins to fix it) or ourselves (I don't know how to fix the damn car) that we're angry at. Stuff happens – and sometimes we even help it happen by ignoring signals that sooner or later we'll need to do something to take care of an impending problem. So now it's "later" – and we need to fix something.

Anger, at a considerably lower intensity than downright PO'd, can be beneficial in that it can help us identify situations that we might want to address – either in an external situation or within ourselves. Anger is not all as bad as some folks would lead us to believe. The important thing is that we recognize its source (that'd be us) and take whatever steps are needed to bring it back under our conscious control. This includes professional counseling if necessary.

Life's too short to for us to eat up a bunch of time being angry. Why don't we all have a super-duper triple-sized banana split instead? Just a thought...

This Just Ain't Good!

"Nope, this just ain't good!" How many times in our lives have we had those or similar words bouncing around inside our skulls? Yeah, I've lost count, too!

There are usually only a few reasons these annoying words show up. Occasionally, it'll be when we just run smack-dab into an "Oh Shit!" situation. You know what I mean. Accidents, diseases and a whole bunch of other stuff that seem to have popped up out of nowhere and suddenly we find ourselves up to our neck in swamp water with alligators nipping at our butts.

Now admittedly, some of these situations that seem to pop up out of nowhere are a normal result of the things we personally did or didn't do. We made our own bed and suddenly we're forced to either lie in it or start ripping off the sheets. Don't ya just hate it when that happens?

Other times, an event occurs that honestly is completely beyond our control. These are just unfortunately part of life. Natural disasters, impulsive or inconsiderate actions by other folks and many diseases fall into this category. Once again, we're put into a position where we'll likely need to do something that we never would have wanted to do in the first place. Dang the bad luck...

In both of these types of situations, we're forced into a position of either having to "act" or suffer the undesirable con-sequences. Most of us will then put our logic and maybe even our survival instincts to work to do those things we need to do to try to overcome our yucky situation. More often than not, we'll succeed. Cool!

But what about those situations that quietly sneak up on you? You know the ones I'm talking about. It's the job that started out to be pretty good and later on down the road has turned into drudgery and uncertainty. The relationship that was once built on caring and compassion which has deteriorated into indifference or abuse. The life path that was once paved and well maintained that has made a gradual transition into a muddy cow path. Now what?

Unfortunately, because the rate of change from "great" to "crappy" was so gradual, we tend to be reasonably well adapted to our present situation even though it may be quite uncomfortable. We may even be resigned to the fact that "this is the way it is" – or feel that we have invested so much time and effort into our circumstances that it just wouldn't be worthwhile to try to make any changes. We feel trapped – and annoyed by those danged words bouncing back and forth inside our heads. "This just ain't good!" "This just ain't good!"

Oh, if only this were one of those sudden "Oh Shit!" situations. If it were only a matter of immediate urgency. Then I'll bet we'd do something. We'd take action and work to overcome our emergency. It'd be a matter of survival!

You don't have to be a psychic to know where I'm going with this, do you? Nah, it's pretty obvious. An uncomfortable condition – whether it suddenly pops into our lives or develops over a period of several years – is still an uncomfortable condition. Yeah, this is one of those "If it looks like a duck, walks like a duck..." well, you know the rest...

And that bring us to our "This Just Ain't Good" checklist. When we find ourselves in uncomfortable or undesirable situations, we only have two initial choices.

1. Do Nothing – This of course, is the easiest course of action and is absolutely guaranteed to bring about zero change. Things will continue to be as they are right now. (Is this the way you really want to finish out your life...?)

2. Do Something – This is the more difficult of the two choices because it immediately creates two more choices.

A.   Take action to change the situation – Change jobs, relationships, life path or whatever condition is causing the discomfort.

B. Take action to change yourself – Your thought processes, the way you view your job, relationships, etc.

That's it!   That's all the more complicated the initial decision-making process is. And yeah, I know that our "do something" may actually wind up being a combination of mod-ifying both ourselves and our situation. And the actual steps we may be required to take to make those changes may be rather involved and take a bunch of time and effort on our part. That's OK – if we're genuinely interested in making a change. That's just the way life is.

Of course, the basic requirement for making any changes – either within our situation or within ourselves – is "Do Something". Take action. Set some goals for the changes we want, decide what we need to do to get there and get crankin'.

So if you're trudging through life with "This just ain't good!" ringing in your head, use the preceding checklist to decide what you really want to do. And above all, ask yourself the question, "Is this really the way I want the rest of my life to be?"

You'll know what you should do…

It's Character that Counts!

It seems to me a man comes into this world with a little ready raw material – himself. His folks can only give him a sort of push, and a mite of teaching, but in the long run what a man becomes is his own problem. There've always been hard times, there've always been wars and troubles – famine, disease, and such-like – and some folks are born with money, some with none. In the end it is up to the man what he becomes, and none of those other things matter. In horses, dogs, and men it is character that counts.

From "Chancy" by Louis L'Amour
Copyright 1968 by Bantam Books, Inc.

I Am...

...you are, he is, she is, they are... But you knew that already, didn't you? Or have you really stopped to think about it recently – or ever for that matter?

Huh?

I guess we need a little clarification on this. So...do this. Touch yourself. That's right, go ahead and touch yourself.

So, what did you feel? Skin? Of course. Maybe some hair? OK. How about warmth? Sure, unless you're standing naked in your back yard in Minnesota in the middle of January. (You really need to get back inside as quickly as possible – and try to cut back on the quantity of hot toddies...)

Unless you're numbed out of your gourd or weren't really paying attention, you felt YOU! So what's so special about that? YOU'RE ALIVE! Honest-to-goodness, really alive! Think about it. For about a zillion years you weren't – alive that is. You did not exist. You were only scattered molecular stardust. You could have been a little part of just about anything you can think of – oak tree, beach, chicken feathers – you name it. (Don't dwell too long on this thought. It can get pretty gross real quick if you let it.)

From the beginning of time, we have been nothing more than a potential biological jigsaw puzzle waiting for assembly. And now – son-of-a-gun, here we are. From two microscopic half-cells merged in a surge of passion, the miracle of genetics has transformed that single cell into a zillion-celled, complex, functioning animal organism.

'Tain't no big deal, you say? It happens every day?

Oh, c'mon, now. It is a mega-deal that happens thousands and thousands of times a day. And – it happens with a terrifically small percentage of errors. As a general rule, our noses, eyes and ears wind up in pretty much the right place on our heads. We have the correct numbers of arms, legs, fingers and toes. And our innards are all positioned normally and function as they were intended. All this from a microscopic cell latched onto the lining of Mom's womb!

Let's take a quick inventory of "us".

We all have a really cool, flexible, articulating framework as a foundation for the rest of the stuff we're made of. Over 200 bones, all connected together and hinged so we can walk, talk, stand, sit, run, bend, stoop, squat, jump, reach, grasp, point, scratch, eat, push, pull, lift, swim, lie down and perform any other maneuver or contortion you can think of. Cool, huh? In addition of course, some of this framework also does a great job of protecting our insides – brain, lungs, heart, and digestive system – from damage from excessive outside forces.

All of these fairly solid hunks of material are connected and maneuvered by our tendons, ligaments and muscles. The assemblies of interconnected, expandable, contractible, cells that work harmoniously as directed to allow us to accomplish all of the things we've already mentioned.

Think about it! Just the fact that we have a solid supporting framework that we can manipulate and move pretty much as we desire is amazing in and of itself!

Our basic building blocks – our cells – are all individually live little bits of protein and goo that use the oxygen and nutrients they are supplied to multiply and do the jobs required of the organ that they are a part of.

Our digestive system takes the raw materials we provide it in the way of food (and occasionally assorted garbage), processes it into a form usable by the cells and ships it out through our internal distribution system. The unusable excess is dumped (excuse the term) externally.

Our circulatory system – heart, arteries, capillaries, veins – transport nourishment, oxygen, and an assortment of other chemicals and substances (hormones, biological warriors, waste materials and occasional invading buggies) to and from all of our body parts (individual cells).

Our respiratory system – lungs and associated passageways – snags the oxygen from the air, passes it along to the transporters in our bloodstream, drags the carbon dioxide (one of the byproducts of cell life) back out of the blood and expels it out into the air.

Our nervous system receives outside stimuli from sights, sounds, smells, tastes and "feels", translates it into generally comprehensible information and either uses it immediately to produce a response or stores it for future reference. At the same time, it keeps all of our internal processes functioning in a fairly efficient manner.

Add to all of this, our systems and sub-systems for gathering the outside stimuli in the first place (eyes, ears, nose, etc.), fighting off disease, healing injuries, maintaining body temperature, maintaining chemical balance, growing hair, producing freckles, passing gas, reproducing, etc., and suddenly we are introduced to ourselves as an extremely complex biological organism!

Hells bells, folks! We are the most complicated assembly of parts and pieces on the face of this earth! We are so complicated in fact, that even after studying our body parts for all these years to try to figure out exactly how all our stuff works, we still don't know everything! Maybe we never will. Who knows?

Are ya trackin' with me here? We – you and I – are ALIVE! We're functioning and doing all the stuff that we human-type animals do. If that's not absolutely mind-boggling, I don't know what is!

To Achieve Your Dreams – Remember Your A, B, C's

Avoid negative sources, people, things and habits.

Believe in yourself.

Consider things from every angle.

Don't give up and don't give in.

Enjoy life today; yesterday is gone and tomorrow may never come.

Family and Friends are hidden treasures. Seek them and enjoy their riches.

Give more than you planned to give.

Hang on to your dreams. **I**gnore those who try to discourage you.

Just do it!

Keep on trying, no matter how hard it seems. It will get better.

Love yourself first and foremost.

Make it happen.

Never lie, cheat, or steal. Always strike a fair deal.

Open your eyes and see things as they really are.

Practice makes perfect.

Quitters never win and winners never quit.

Read, study and learn about everything important in your life.

Stop procrastinating.

Take control of your own destiny.

Understand yourself in order to better understand others.

Visualize it.

Want it more than anything.

Xccelerate your efforts. **X**pect good things to happen.

You are unique of all Nature's creations. Nothing can replace you.

Zero in on your target, and go for it!!

Life's an Illusion

I'll get right to the point. Life is not necessarily what we think it is. And no, I'm not going to extrapolate this to the extreme to try to convince you that we really exist on some obscure planet in a distant spiral galaxy and that all of this we're experiencing as "Life" is only a dream. Of course, it is kind of cool to think that we could waking up any time now, wandering out to the kptfrun to put on the cuggy and then stepping out on the prafo to watch the bos rise and enjoy the sounds of the bilbs as they greet the morning. We naturally, would be all the more enlightened because of the dream experience of the previous night and could therefore anticipate an even more productive, enjoyable day at the Snark assembly plant. (Does excessive caffeine intake cause everyone to think weird stuff like that? Probably just me, huh?)

Where were we? Oh yeah, the illusion thing... Let's start with the physical, material stuff. Everything you see is not as it appears – or as it is interpreted by our little brains. When we look around, we "see" all kinds of solid forms. Computers, desks, paper, chairs, walls, books, etc. These things not only look solid, they feel solid and can be held, moved, sat upon, used to support other solid things - and broken. So they're all composed of some densely packed material and therefore are completely "solid", right?

Not even close, Martha. When you get down to the itty bitty particles that all of these nice solid objects are made of, you're gonna find only little teeny tiny bits of energy, specks of particles and a hell of a lot of space between them. In fact, there's a bunch more space than there are specks of particles. Here's one of the analogies I can relate to easily. If we arbitrarily designated the nucleus of an atom (the combination of the neutrons and protons in the center of an atom that contain just about all of the atom's mass) as the size of a grapefruit, the rest of the atom that is the electron cloud (little negatively charged particles that are zipping around the nucleus like a bat outta hell) would take up a space equivalent to a large football stadium. Hmm, let's see. Grapefruit is the "solid" stuff – football stadium is the space and energy stuff. Yeah, there's a hell of a lot of space inside those little atom guys.

Of course, when these little bundles of specks and energy (it would take about a hundred million of 'em laid end to end to stretch out to a length of approximately one centimeter) share their electrons to bond with another atom – or atoms – to form molecules... and then these molecules link together using the energy of their foundation atoms, we can wind up with materials that appear and act like they're completely solid. OK, for those of you who may tend to get picky here, we also wind up with other similar things we can touch such as gas (air) and liquid – the other two states of matter that make up our world.

So where's that leave us? Surrounded by, living with, eating, drinking, using and yes, even mating with "things" that are mostly space and energy. (I think I just saw several married ladies' hands go up to question the energy part of that last statement. Please put your hands down. You know what I mean...)

Our physical, material world then is not exactly what we normally perceive it to be. And, if you've been tracking along with me through the previous chapters, it's fairly easy to see that the rest of our little world operates pretty much along those same lines. Our perceptions of ourselves, of those around us and the events and situations in our lives and the rest of the world are shaped primarily by our inputs and experiences to this point in our lives. Depending on the "quality" of our programming so far, our personal perceptions of this world can range from fairly realistic to way outta whack. The great thing about this though, is that other's perceptions of our perceptions are tinted by their own personal or collective experiences (programming) so as a result, reality (if there is such a thing) clouds up really quick. Whoa... I think I just gave myself a headache

Yes, it's often extremely difficult to determine where skewed perception ends and reality begins. Of one thing we can be sure.

Our individual perceptions of life are the foundations for our personal reality. So I'll encourage you once again. If your reality is not everything you desire – if it's not bringing you the enjoyment of life you feel you deserve – then it's worth putting forth a little effort to examine your "programming" to see if there aren't a few changes you'd like to make in your thought processes and the way you're viewing life. It can be well worth the effort.

While you're doing that, I really do need to get rid of my headache. I think I'll pour a cup of cuggy and go out on the prafo to watch the bos rise...

The Truth about Hugs

Just a little reminder about one of the more important things in life…

There's no such thing as a bad hug, only good ones and great ones.

Hugs are nonfattening and they don't cause cancer or cavities.

Hugs are all natural with no preservatives, artificial ingredients or pesticide residue.

Hugs are cholesterol-free, naturally sweet, 100% wholesome and they are a completely renewable resource.

Hugs are easy to care for, they don't require batteries, tune-ups, or x-rays.

Hugs are non-taxable, fully returnable and energy efficient.

Hugs are safe in all kinds of weather…

In fact, hugs are especially good for cold and rainy days and -

Hugs are exceptionally effective in treating problems like bad dreams or Monday blues...

Never wait until tomorrow to hug someone you could hug today, because when you give one, you get one right back your way!

Now stop reading and go hug someone awready!

So What is Success Anyway?

Well I'll tell you what it's not. Even though many of us like to periodically visit our own personal Fantasyland complete with its mansions, servants, fancy cars and trips to exotic places (check under the heading of "What I Would Do if I Won the Lottery") most of us over the age of twelve with any experience under our belts are realistic enough to recognize our Fantasyland for what it is. A fun place to visit but one sorely lacking in personal fulfillment.

Unfortunately, there are many in our society who have bought into the concept that equates "success" with big money. And you can't really blame them. Our entertainment industry and the media have vigorously promoted this concept. "Join us now as we take a closer look at the lifestyles of the rich and famous!" "Travel in luxurious style in our Really Expensive Vehicle!" "Are you ready to be a Success? I made a million dollars last year and you can do the same!" "Dress for Success with this Really Expensive Suit from the Really Expensive Store!"

OK, all of you with a huge checking account and a pile of assets can just relax and take a deep breath. I personally feel that anyone who has worked hard and has earned their money honestly is deserving of at least a pat on the back. There's a good chance that a lot of people have benefited in one way or another from your efforts. That's another checkmark in the plus column.

So yes, money can be an indication of – or a result of – success. But it ain't "success".

So what is success anyway? Here's old Gene's personal opinion. Success is simply taking the steps to do the things you want to do. And it doesn't matter what those "things" are. It can be just being the best mom or dad possible. Or being the best teacher or secretary or tree-trimmer or banjo player or dog groomer or volunteer that you can possibly be. And no, you don't need to be better than anyone else at what you like to do. Just working to be the best you can be – at whatever interests you - immediately qualifies you as a huge SUCCESS!

So don't waste the time and energy trying to compare yourself – that unique, special "you" – to anyone else. Don't drive yourself bonkers trying to live up to what you may see as another person's success. It's not a valid comparison and it's just not worth the effort. Instead, focus on what you want to do – what you want to accomplish in life. If you'll set this image in your head and work for it, you can immediately consider yourself to be "successful". In fact, maybe you should get a plaque or poster that says "I'm Successful!" and place it in some highly visible spot in your house or apartment. What the heck. You deserve it!

Setting Goals – Things to Think About

We hear a lot about the steps we should take to achieve our goals, however unless we take the first steps to realistically consider who and what we are right now – our capabilities and interests – and think logically about what we'd like to accomplish, our chances of achieving our "goal" are slim to none. Here are a few things to think about when you're trying to decide what you'd like to do.

1. Your goals need to be your goals
Not your spouse's or significant other's, not your friends', parents', children's, etc. - YOURS!

2. Your goals must be achievable
It's great to stretch for them, in fact it's desirable, but you must be able to honestly picture yourself achieving them.

3. You must be willing to put forth some extra effort
It's not possible to achieve more by vegging out in front of the TV. It will take extra effort and sometimes extra money.

"You can't take a trip unless you're willing to pay the price of the ticket."

4. You gotta really want to do it
How can you achieve something you really don't want? If you can honestly picture yourself doing this "thing" you want to do and can approach the task of getting it done with a positive attitude, your chances for success are very good.

*Success - taking the steps to do those things you want to do!

5. Be picky about who you tell
We need positives and support to accomplish our goals. Share your thoughts and plans only with those who will back your efforts.

6. Achieving your goal must benefit everyone concerned

Think about the end result of achieving your goal. How will others be affected? Will the overall result be positive and in everyone's best interests?

(Note: Not everyone has to <u>like</u> the result!)

7. Will accomplishing your goal be fun/enjoyable?

There can be some hard work between "here" and "there". If we get satisfaction from our progress and we know we'll feel good when we reach our goal, we'll have a much better chance of getting it done.

(Why would we ever do anything to intentionally make our lives miserable?)

One last thing. OK, maybe a couple of last things. The two references to imaging – as in being able to "picture" yourself achieving your goal – are extremely important. The picture you create is far more powerful than any words you could ever use to describe a goal. It should be an integral part of the initial thinking and planning process. Also – spend a little time thinking about the PEMS sisters. You know what I'm talking about, right? The Physical, Emotional, Mental and Spiritual components of our life that are a part of everything we do? Include them as partners in the planning of your new life video. You may just find that one of them will turn out to be the deciding factor in whether or not you should move into the full production process.

To succeed – just do what you love to do.

A Quick Checklist for Improving Your Life

1. Learn About You

If you don't know who you are and why you think and act the way you do, it's gonna be really difficult to make any positive changes in your life. Take a look first at your parents and close family members. Think about how they look and how they deal with life. This is the basis for who you are today. You've been instilled with the tendency to think as they think and act as they act. It's just the way it is.

Now think about the big events in your life so far. The ones that stand out in your mind. The ones that made an impression – negative or positive – on you. These events have likely influenced how you think and act today. Oh sure, we can add in every little thing that you've ever seen, heard, felt, smelled or touched because "everything" has had some effect on you - on how you think and deal with life. But it's the "biggies" that usually have the most impact.

You can write some of this down if you want to. Make a list of things you like or don't like. Things you enjoy doing. Things that make you happy or sad. But you don't need to if you'd rather not. Just thinking about this is a major step in the right direction. Just get to know you. It's important.

2. Learn About Others

You already know now why you are you. Think about why other people think and act as they do. It should be fairly simple because they're who and what they are for the same reasons you are who you are. They've just had a different family and life experiences. Therefore, they'll all act at least somewhat differently – and think differently – than you. Why spend the time learning about others? Well because – the more you learn about why other folks think and act as they do, the more you'll learn about yourself. And that's still important.

3. Practice Thinking Differently

If you continue to think the same way as you do right now, nothing can change. Everything we do is based on how we think – about ourselves, about others and about life. If you think life is pretty crappy, well sure enough, it'll be pretty crappy. If you think life is generally OK, sure enough, it'll be generally OK. If you think you're a loser, you are. If you think you have a lot to offer your friends, family and this world, you do. We think our way to our destiny. What's your destiny?

4. Pour a Solid Foundation

You can't build much of anything without a strong foundation structure. Roads, buildings, bridges, cars, life – all require a firm foundation to last and withstand the eroding elements of nature. If you haven't already, you might consider looking into using a spiritually-based concrete for your foundation. (No, I didn't say religious, but if that's your preference, use it.) Strong values and principles can provide reinforcement. If you'll continue to work to add strength to your under-footing as you go through life, you'll have all the support you'll ever need.

5. Build a New Life

Use whatever references you think you need to start – and continue – your building process. There are plenty of organizations, schools and references of all types available to help you on your way. Find the experts and listen to their stories and advice. Identify a mentor, coach or a close friend who can give you lots of support and encouragement. And be sure to DO SOMETHING! ACT! All the information and knowledge is worthless unless you put it to work for you. Decide what you would like your destiny to be. Then just go for it!

I hope you have a really great life!

JUST GO FOR IT!

About the author:

His name is Gene. He likes to help people - so he does.

Apart from that, Gene's life experiences span well over 60 years. Beginning on a small farm in the fertile Platte River valley of central Nebraska, his wanderings have taken him through college, the military, two major corporations and into the field of instruction in both the private and public sector.

For the past twenty plus years, he has devoted much of his time to the study and understanding of the nature (and peculiarities) of mankind and its place and purpose in the universe.

He shares with you now, the results of his studies so far, in the hopes that he "can help make just one person's life a little easier – and a little more fun".

Other books by Gene Simmons available from NuPathz:

Is This As Good As It Gets?
Sometimes life deals us a mediocre hand, then apparently changes the rules of the game without warning. It presents uncomfortable situations, yet seemingly offers little in the way of solutions. Life tears at our hearts and our minds, beating us down physically, mentally, emotionally and spiritually.

Is this really the life we were intended to experience? Or is our life just an uncomfortable result of the things we have learned from our experiences and people that have been an influential part of our lives so far?

In slightly over 50 pages, Gene reveals some of the basic rules of Life that, if put to use, will make a dramatic difference in how you view life - and in your approach to making those improvements you'd like to make. Discover now, your path to a fulfilling, truly enjoyable lifestyle!

Just Between us Critters
We're strange creatures...and we continue to prove it by periodically doing some really strange things. Things that are dictated not so much by logical thought processes as by a "gut reaction" to a given situation.

How can we as intelligent, civilized human beings do so many things that wind up costing us so much money, creating so much conflict and getting us into so much trouble?

Are we just warped? Unbalanced? Weird? Misguided? Under a spell? Sinful?

Or – are our actions just being heavily influenced by some basic animal instinct? By our mental design and programming that help assure our survival as individuals and as a species?

Discover the possible causes of many of our personal and collective conflicts. Learn how our instincts can impact our daily lives and frequently even totally control the things we do.

What Am I Doing Here?

So what's going on in your life? Everything calm and kick-back? Relaxed and easy? Got it all under control? Yeah, I know. Gimme a break! It's like "what planet are you from, Bozo?" So just why the heck are we going through what we're going through? Why are we having these weird things happen to us? What's with this "supernatural" stuff anyway? And what's with most of the rest of the world? Is everybody just goofy?

In just over 50 pages, Gene offers several possible answers to some of life's biggest questions. Answers that can make a world of difference in how you view life –and how much you enjoy the time you're spending on this old earth.

Up Close and Personal

We're making this much too difficult. Somewhere along the way, we got the strange idea that it is really difficult to talk with God. How did that happen? How did something so easy, so normal, so natural, get so screwed up?

We poor, misguided humans have become so entrenched, so enamored with our self-imposed rules and traditions that we have damn near lost our ability to communicate with the single entity that is responsible for our very existence. Does that make a lick of sense to anyone?

Wouldn't it be really nice to be able to just relax and BS with God – no matter who we are or what we've done? Wouldn't it be great to be able to really talk with him and his helpers – and know that they'll be doing things that can actually help us and make our lives easier?

Learn about some of the techniques you can use to do exactly that. Find out how cool God really is!

* NuPathz *

http://www.nupathz.com/

Your affordable source for self improvement and self help books & materials!

Bringing you a new perspective on life!

Don't settle for anything less than a SUPER life!
Let NuPathz help you "Get Your Butt Outta the Rut!"

www.ingramcontent.com/pod-product-compliance
Lightning Source LLC
Chambersburg PA
CBHW020351290526
45785CB00005B/2235